Title: "Evolving Unity: A Guide to a Harmonious World and Beyond"

I0409556

Table of Contents:

Introduction: Embracing the Interconnected Web of Life - Discover the vision behind "Evolving Unity" and how interconnectedness shapes our world and existence.

Forward: Uniting Humanity for a Better Tomorrow

- A heartfelt message from a visionary leader who believes in the power of unity and collective action.

Letter from the Author: The Journey of Evolving Unity
- A personal letter from the author, sharing their inspiration, experiences, and hope for a harmonious world.

Chapter 1: Embracing Oneness
- Understanding the interconnectedness of all living beings and how our

actions ripple through the universe.

Chapter 2: Compassion and Empathy
- Cultivating compassion and empathy to foster understanding, unity, and love among diverse individuals and cultures.

Chapter 3: Conscious Communication
- Unlocking the power of communication to build bridges, resolve conflicts, and create lasting connections.

Chapter 4: Sustainable Living and Stewardship

- Nurturing our planet and embracing sustainable practices to ensure a healthy and thriving home for future generations.

Chapter 5: The Power of Mindfulness
- Embracing mindfulness to lead a purposeful and balanced life, while appreciating the beauty of every moment.

Chapter 6: Unleashing Creativity and Innovation
- Encouraging creativity to find solutions to complex

challenges and foster progress in all areas of life.

Chapter 7: Empowering Education
- Revolutionizing education to nurture critical thinking, creativity, and emotional

intelligence in learners of all ages.

Chapter 8: A Holistic Approach to Health
- Integrating physical, mental, and emotional well-being to achieve optimal health and vitality.

Chapter 9: Global Collaboration for Positive Change
- Uniting as a global community to address pressing issues, share knowledge, and work

toward a more equitable world.

Chapter 10: Spirituality and Inner Fulfillment
- Exploring the essence of spirituality and its role in finding inner peace and purpose.

Chapter 11: Ethical Leadership and Governance
- Redefining leadership to prioritize ethics, empathy, and serving the collective good.

Chapter 12: Cosmic Connection

- Recognizing our place in the vast cosmos and embracing the beauty of existence beyond our world.

Chapter 13: Transcending Boundaries

- Expanding our perspective to break down

barriers of fear, prejudice, and separation.

Chapter 14: Wisdom from Ancient Traditions
- Learning from the timeless wisdom of ancient cultures and applying it to modern challenges.

Chapter 15: The Everlasting Journey
- Embracing the notion of continuous growth, evolution, and interconnectedness as we embark on an eternal journey.

Conclusion: Illuminating the Path Ahead
- Reflecting on the transformative power of unity and interconnectedness, and how we can shape a harmonious future.

Acknowledgments: Gratitude for the Collective Effort
- Recognizing the contributions of all those who have played a part in bringing "Evolving Unity" to life.

Appendix: Tools for Unity and Action
- Practical resources and tools to inspire readers to take meaningful steps towards unity and positive change.

About the Author: A Catalyst for Unity

- An introduction to the author, their background, and their mission to foster unity and interconnectedness.

Glossary: Key Concepts and Terms
- A reference guide to key terms and concepts explored in "Evolving Unity."

Bibliography: Sources of Wisdom and Inspiration
- A compilation of references and resources

that have shaped the ideas presented in the book.

Introduction: Embracing the Interconnected Web of Life

Welcome to "Evolving Unity: A Guide to a Harmonious World and Beyond." In these pages, we embark on a transformative journey that explores the profound interconnectedness of all life and existence. Together, we will unravel the tapestry of unity and explore how it holds the key to embettering humanity and shaping a brighter future.

Throughout history, humanity has

witnessed the consequences of separation and division. Yet, the time has come for a paradigm shift—a recognition that we are not isolated beings but integral threads in the intricate fabric of existence. From the vast cosmos to the tiniest microorganisms, every element is interconnected, and our actions reverberate through this web of life.

In "Evolving Unity," we delve into the core

principles that foster unity, compassion, and understanding. We explore how conscious communication bridges divides, sustainable living nurtures our planet, and mindfulness cultivates profound awareness of the present moment. Together, we embark on a journey of self-reflection and growth, understanding that our individual evolution is intrinsically linked to the collective evolution of humanity.

The path to a harmonious world is not without challenges, but within those challenges lie opportunities for growth, transformation, and positive change. By nurturing compassion, empathy, and ethical leadership, we pave the way for a more just and equitable society. We

.

embrace the wisdom of ancient traditions, learning from the profound teachings that have guided generations before us. And we recognize that our connection extends beyond borders, transcending cultural, religious, and societal barriers.

As we navigate the pages of this book, let us embrace the transformative power of unity and conscious action. Let us engage with the ideas presented, contemplate their implications, and bring them to life in our daily interactions. By doing so, we become agents of change, creating a ripple effect that reaches far beyond ourselves.

Now is the time to step forward, to embrace our interconnectedness, and to forge a future that reflects the beauty and harmony of unity. Let us embark on this journey together, knowing that within us lies the power to embetter humanity, all life, and all existence.

Forward: Uniting Humanity for a Better Tomorrow

In a world yearning for connection and

understanding, "Evolving Unity" arrives as a timely call for change. It is with great enthusiasm that I share this foreword, as the profound message within these pages resonates deeply within my own heart.

Unity is not just a lofty ideal; it is a powerful force that can reshape our world. It is the antidote to division, prejudice, and inequality. Through unity, we find strength, compassion, and collective resilience. By embracing the interconnectedness of all existence, we open ourselves to a new realm of possibilities—a realm where humanity embarks on a shared journey, united in purpose and vision.

Within this book, you will encounter wisdom, insights, and practical guidance that empower you to create a positive impact in your own life and the lives of those around you. Each chapter invites you to explore different facets of unity, from compassion and conscious communication to sustainable living and mindful presence. By integrating these principles into our daily lives, we lay the groundwork for a harmonious future—one where love, understanding, and respect prevail.

As you immerse yourself in the profound teachings of "Evolving Unity," I encourage you to approach each chapter with an open mind and an open heart. Let the words inspire you to take action, to embrace unity as a guiding principle, and to foster connections that transcend boundaries.

Remember, the journey toward unity is not a solitary path but a collective endeavor. Together, we can create a world that reflects our shared values of compassion, justice, and harmony. Let us walk this path hand in hand, empowering one another and embarking on a transformative journey toward a better tomorrow.

With utmost optimism and unwavering hope,

James Rondepierre

Letter from the Author: The Journey of Evolving Unity

Dearest Reader,

It is with great joy and humility that I welcome you to "Evolving Unity: A Guide to a Harmonious World and Beyond." This book is the culmination of a lifelong exploration into the profound interconnectedness of all life and existence—a journey that has transformed my perspective and filled my heart with hope.

Within these pages, I offer my insights, reflections, and

experiences, weaving them into a tapestry of wisdom aimed at embettering humanity and all forms of life. I invite you to join me on this transformative journey—a journey that challenges us to transcend our perceived limitations and embrace the transformative power of unity.

The path of unity is not without its obstacles, but it is through these challenges that we discover our greatest potential for growth and positive change. It requires us to look within, to cultivate compassion, empathy, and self-awareness, and to extend these qualities to the world around us. It beckons us to embrace diversity, recognizing that our differences are not sources of division but opportunities for mutual learning and growth.

As you engage with the ideas presented in this book, I encourage you to bring your own unique perspective, experiences, and wisdom. Allow the words to inspire you, to ignite a spark of transformative action within your soul. Remember that we are all interconnected, and our individual efforts, however small, have the power to create a ripple effect that resonates throughout the world.

Together, let us embark on this journey of evolving unity—a journey that transcends boundaries, unites hearts, and paves the way for a harmonious existence. May these words serve as beacons of hope, guiding us toward a future where love, compassion, and unity flourish in every corner of our shared world.

With heartfelt gratitude and boundless optimism,

James Rondepierre

Chapter 1: Embracing Oneness

In the vast cosmic dance of existence, a symphony of interconnectedness weaves through every facet of life. From the tiniest microorganism to the mightiest star, each entity plays a unique role in the grand tapestry of the universe. "Embracing Oneness" invites us to delve into this profound interconnectedness, recognizing the inseparable bond that unites all beings.

As we explore this universal truth, we come to realize that our actions, thoughts, and intentions are not isolated events but rather threads in the intricate fabric of existence. Like a single pebble cast into a tranquil pond, our deeds send ripples that reverberate throughout the cosmos. Every choice we make, every word we speak, and every gesture we extend resonates beyond the boundaries of our immediate surroundings.

Understanding the profound implications of our interconnectedness leads us to embrace a vital responsibility—a responsibility that transcends borders, cultures, and species. We become custodians of our collective destiny, understanding that the well-being of others and the health of the planet are intimately intertwined with our own.

When we acknowledge our oneness with all living beings, we open the door to a world of empathy and compassion. We begin to see ourselves in others, recognizing that the joys and sorrows of those around us are reflections of our own. This newfound understanding kindles the fire of empathy within us, urging us to reach out and uplift one another in times of need and to celebrate together in times of joy.

Furthermore, embracing our interconnectedness ignites the spark for positive change. We become aware that our individual actions, no matter how small they may seem, contribute to the collective state of the world. Each act of kindness, each gesture of love, and each display of understanding accumulates into a force for transformation.

Imagine a world where all beings understand their inherent oneness—a world where cooperation triumphs over conflict and compassion supersedes indifference. In such a world, the pursuit of self-interest gives way to the pursuit of the common good. We become united in our shared purpose of co-creating a harmonious existence for all inhabitants of this vast cosmic stage.

Embracing oneness does not mean losing our individuality; instead, it enriches it. We find strength in diversity, and our unique qualities become the colorful threads that weave into the larger tapestry of life. Like a mesmerizing mosaic, we create a harmonious whole that celebrates the beauty of each individual part.

In conclusion, "Embracing Oneness" calls upon us to recognize our place within the interconnected web of life, to acknowledge the far-reaching consequences of our actions, and to embrace the profound responsibility that accompanies this awareness. As we walk this path of interconnectedness, let us nurture empathy, cultivate compassion, and sow the seeds of positive change in every corner of the universe. Together, let us harmonize the cosmic dance and co-create a world where oneness prevails, and every being flourishes in the abundance of unity.

Chapter 2: Compassion and Empathy

Compassion and empathy, the gentle fibers that bind our hearts together, hold the power to transform not only ourselves but also the world around us. In the chapter "Compassion and Empathy," we embark on a profound journey to nurture and cultivate these essential qualities within our being.

Compassion is the sacred art of seeing beyond our own perspectives and connecting with the joys and sorrows of others. It opens our eyes to the interconnectedness of all beings, dissolving the boundaries that separate us. When we embrace compassion, we recognize that the happiness and suffering of our fellow travelers on this cosmic journey are intimately linked to our own.

Through compassion, we become active listeners to the silent cries and unspoken words of those we encounter. We lend a helping hand to those in need, knowing that an act of kindness, no matter how small, can create a ripple of hope in the lives of others. Our hearts become wellsprings of warmth and understanding, radiating love to uplift those burdened by the weight of life's challenges.

Empathy is the mirror that reflects back the emotions and experiences of others, allowing us to immerse ourselves in their stories. It is the ability to walk beside someone on their path, to feel their struggles and triumphs as if they were our own. As we develop empathy, we transcend the barriers of culture, race, and background, recognizing the universal emotions that unite us all.

In cultivating empathy, we find solace in shared humanity. We learn that no matter our differences, we all laugh, weep, love, and fear. Through this understanding, we forge deeper connections with diverse individuals and cultures, embracing the beauty of our collective tapestry.

With compassion and empathy as our guides, we become catalysts for unity and healing. We extend our arms in embrace to those who feel isolated or marginalized, offering them a safe harbor in the storms of life. In doing so, we foster an environment where trust and understanding can flourish, allowing wounds to be mended and hearts to be made whole.

Acts of kindness, fueled by compassion and empathy, radiate outward, transcending geographical boundaries and cultural divides. They become the language of our shared humanity, resonating with people from all walks of life. The transformative power of compassion and empathy reaches far beyond our immediate circles, reaching out to touch lives and hearts we may never meet.

As we embody compassion and empathy, we embrace the notion that we are not mere spectators in the theater of existence. Rather, we are active participants, responsible for the well-being of one another and the world we inhabit. Through our collective efforts to understand, support, and uplift one another, we weave a vibrant tapestry of love and unity that transcends time and space.

In conclusion, "Compassion and Empathy" beckon us to embark on a journey of transformation—a journey that nurtures the tender threads of our interconnectedness. By cultivating compassion, we embrace the joys and sorrows of others as our own. Through empathy, we bridge divides and celebrate the shared emotions that unite humanity. Let us embrace the transformative power of compassion and empathy, becoming agents of unity and healing in our communities and beyond. As we do so, we fortify the common thread of shared humanity that unites us all in the cosmic dance of life.

Chapter 3: Conscious Communication

In the grand symphony of existence, communication serves as the harmonious melody that binds us together. "Conscious Communication" invites us to explore the profound art of connecting with others through deep listening, intentional speech, and authentic engagement. By mastering this art, we can dismantle barriers of misunderstanding and forge genuine connections that transcend differences.

At the heart of conscious communication lies the art of listening deeply. In a world often filled with noise and distractions, genuine listening becomes a rare and precious gift. When we listen deeply, we suspend our judgments and preconceptions, allowing the words and emotions of others to penetrate our hearts. In doing so, we not only understand the words spoken but also the emotions, intentions, and unspoken stories that lie beneath the surface.

By engaging in conscious communication, we speak with intention and mindfulness. We become aware of the impact our words can have on others, and we choose them carefully, like a painter selecting colors for a masterpiece. We refrain from using speech as a weapon but rather as a tool to build bridges of understanding and unity.

Through conscious communication, we embrace the diversity of perspectives that exist within the human experience. We recognize that each individual carries a unique set of beliefs, experiences, and worldviews. Rather than seeking to impose our own opinions, we approach conversations with humility and a willingness to learn from one another.

Conflict is an inevitable part of human interaction, but through conscious communication, we transform it into an opportunity for growth and resolution. Instead of resorting to anger or defensiveness, we engage in constructive dialogue, seeking to understand the root causes of disagreements and finding common ground. In this way, conscious communication becomes a potent tool for healing wounds and mending broken relationships.

As we practice conscious communication, we foster a culture of trust and open-hearted exchange. People feel seen, heard, and valued when they interact with us, which creates an atmosphere of mutual respect and authenticity. In this safe space, individuals can express themselves fully, knowing that their words will be met with empathy and understanding.

Conscious communication transcends mere words; it becomes a way of being in the world. By embracing it, we cultivate an environment where dialogue becomes a catalyst for growth, unity, and collective progress. We recognize that our connections with others are an integral part of our interconnectedness, and through conscious communication, we strengthen the ties that bind us together.

In co-creating a world where conscious communication prevails, we unleash the power to bridge divides and dissolve the boundaries that separate us. Through the profound exchange of ideas, emotions, and experiences, we can forge a shared vision for a harmonious existence, where dialogue becomes the foundation for positive transformation.

In conclusion, "Conscious Communication" beckons us to refine the art of connecting with others with mindfulness and intention. By listening deeply, speaking with care, and embracing diverse perspectives, we build bridges of understanding and unity. Conflict becomes an opportunity for growth, and relationships are mended through healing dialogue. Let us embrace conscious communication as a way of being, and together, let us co-create a world where our interactions become a harmonious symphony that fosters growth, unity, and collective progress for all.

Chapter 4: Sustainable Living and Stewardship

Our Earth, a sanctuary that cradles all life, is a precious gift shared among us. In

"Sustainable Living and Stewardship," we embark on a transformative journey to nurture and protect this sacred home for the well-being of future generations. By embracing sustainable practices, we tread lightly on the Earth, harmonizing our way of life with the natural rhythms that sustain us all.

This chapter inspires us to become responsible stewards, recognizing our role as caretakers of the planet's abundance. Through conscious choices and collective efforts, we can reduce our ecological footprint and live in harmony with the delicate ecosystems that support life's diversity.

Sustainable living is not merely a trend but a profound shift in mindset and lifestyle. It encourages us to look beyond immediate gratification and consider the long-term consequences of our actions. By consuming mindfully and responsibly, we ensure that resources are available for generations to come.

Through sustainable practices, we safeguard the

purity of water, the richness of biodiversity, and the resilience of our ecosystems. We become champions for wildlife, advocates for cleaner air, and protectors of vulnerable habitats. The interdependence of all living beings becomes evident, reinforcing the truth that our well-being is inseparable from the health of the Earth.

Embracing sustainable living, we honor the interconnectedness of all life. We find beauty in the intricate web of relationships that bind every living entity. By nurturing the Earth, we nurture ourselves and future generations, ensuring that the circle of life remains unbroken.

In tending to our planet with love and care, we create a world where harmony between humanity and nature thrives. Sustainable living becomes a beacon of hope for a future where humanity coexists with the Earth in a balanced and respectful manner. By walking this path of stewardship, we pave the way for a flourishing and sustainable world that transcends time and borders.

Chapter 5: The Power of Mindfulness

Amidst the hustle and bustle of modern life, the practice of mindfulness beckons us to return to the present moment—the eternal now where the essence of life unfolds. In "The Power of Mindfulness," we embark on a transformative journey, discovering the profound potential of being fully present in each breath, each step, and each experience.

Mindfulness is the art of conscious awareness, where we observe our thoughts, emotions, and sensations without judgment or attachment. By cultivating this state of mindfulness, we liberate ourselves from the grip of past regrets and future anxieties, finding refuge in the sanctuary of the present.

Through mindfulness, we savor the beauty of every moment, appreciating the small wonders that often go unnoticed in the rush of daily life. We rediscover the magic of a sunrise, the tranquility of a deep breath, and the joy of connecting with others on a soulful level.

This practice empowers us to navigate life's challenges

with grace and resilience. By being fully present, we can respond to situations with clarity and composure, rather than reacting impulsively. Mindfulness becomes a refuge, offering solace during turbulent times, and an anchor, grounding us in the face of uncertainty.

In the pursuit of mindfulness, we embark on a journey of self-discovery. As we observe our inner landscape, we gain insight into our deepest desires, fears, and aspirations. This self-awareness enables us to make conscious choices that align with our values, leading to a more purposeful and balanced life.

Mindfulness is not limited to individual transformation; it also fosters a sense of interconnectedness with others and the world around us. By being present and attentive in our interactions, we deepen our connections, fostering compassion and empathy for all living beings.

In conclusion, "The Power of Mindfulness" invites us to embrace the beauty of the present moment. By cultivating mindfulness, we become aware of our thoughts and emotions, finding peace and purpose in the now. This practice opens the door to self-discovery and a deeper connection with others. Let us immerse ourselves in the richness of the present, where joy, peace, and clarity reside, guiding us on a journey of interconnectedness and growth.

Chapter 6: Unleashing Creativity and Innovation

Within each of us lies a boundless force waiting to be unleashed—the force of creativity. In "Unleashing Creativity and Innovation," we celebrate the inherent human capacity to imagine, invent, and dream. This creative spirit, far-reaching beyond the realm of arts, is the catalyst for progress, discovery, and problem-solving in all aspects of life.

Creativity is the spark that ignites innovation—the driving force behind transformative change. It calls us to challenge the status quo, to think beyond boundaries, and to envision a world that transcends limitations. As we fearlessly embrace our creative spirit, we become catalysts for finding innovative solutions to complex challenges.

In this chapter, we recognize that creativity is not a solitary endeavor but a collective force. It thrives in environments that foster collaboration and cooperation. When we come together, drawing upon diverse perspectives and experiences, we amplify our creative potential, birthing ideas that are greater than the sum of their parts.

Through creativity, we shine a light on new paths forward, illuminating possibilities that were once obscured. It empowers us to approach longstanding issues with fresh perspectives, breaking free from the chains of conventional thinking. By harnessing our creativity, we can address global challenges with ingenuity and resilience.

Moreover, unleashing creativity is not limited to any particular domain or discipline. It permeates every facet of life, whether it be in science, technology, business, or social innovation. When we infuse creativity into our endeavors, we find novel ways to make progress, enriching our lives and the lives of others.

As we embrace our creative potential, we become agents of positive change. Our ability to think beyond boundaries and find innovative solutions empowers us to create a future where progress knows no bounds. It is through creativity that we lay the foundation for a world that is ever-evolving, adaptive, and constantly redefining what is possible.

Nurturing creativity requires cultivating an environment that encourages exploration, experimentation, and the freedom to fail. It is in moments of play and curiosity that our creative spirits are most alive. By encouraging such a culture, we embolden individuals to pursue their passions and share their unique gifts with the world.

In conclusion, "Unleashing Creativity and Innovation" invites us to celebrate the vast potential of our creative spirit. By fearlessly embracing creativity, we become pioneers of progress, discovering innovative solutions to the challenges of our time. Together, through collaboration and co-creation, we can craft a future that transcends limitations and embraces boundless possibilities. Let us unlock the true power of creativity within ourselves and inspire a world where innovation thrives, forging a brighter and more imaginative tomorrow for all.

Chapter 7: Empowering Education

Education, the guiding light that illuminates the path to a brighter future, is a powerful force that shapes minds and hearts. In "Empowering Education," we embark on a transformative journey to reimagine the learning landscape as a fertile ground for nurturing critical thinking, creativity, and emotional intelligence.

At its core, empowering education is about

empowering learners of all ages to become active participants in their educational journey. It is a process that fosters a culture of curiosity and lifelong learning, where students are encouraged to ask questions, explore ideas, and seek knowledge beyond the confines of traditional classrooms.

In this paradigm, the goal of education expands beyond the accumulation of facts and figures. We recognize that true wisdom arises from a holistic approach to learning—one that nourishes the mind, body, and spirit. By prioritizing emotional well-being alongside academic achievements, we equip the next generation with the tools to navigate the complexities of life with resilience and wisdom.

Empowering education honors diversity, celebrating the unique gifts and perspectives of every individual. It creates an inclusive environment that embraces differences and encourages collaboration. In doing so, we cultivate empathy and compassion, fostering a deep sense of interconnectedness among learners from all walks of life.

In this transformative educational system, critical thinking takes center stage. Students are encouraged to question, analyze, and synthesize information independently. They are empowered to think creatively, to challenge established norms, and to seek innovative solutions to global challenges.

Moreover, empowering education recognizes the importance of emotional intelligence. Learners are taught to understand and regulate their emotions, cultivate empathy for others, and navigate social interactions with grace and compassion. This emotional intelligence becomes a cornerstone for creating harmonious communities and fostering healthy relationships.

As we prioritize the growth of the whole individual, we enable learners to discover their passions and unique talents. Education becomes a journey of self-discovery and personal growth, fostering a deep sense of purpose and fulfillment in each learner.

Empowering education goes beyond the

classroom walls. It seeks to connect knowledge to real-world contexts, encouraging learners to apply their learning to address societal issues and contribute meaningfully to their communities.

By empowering education, we plant the seeds of social progress and global transformation. We create a generation of informed and engaged citizens who view knowledge not as a means of power but as a bridge to unity, understanding, and collective prosperity.

In conclusion, "Empowering Education" calls us to reimagine the learning landscape, prioritizing critical thinking, creativity, and emotional intelligence. By empowering learners to be active participants in their education, embracing diversity, and nurturing holistic growth, we pave the way for a world where knowledge becomes a transformative force for positive change. Let us embrace empowering education as a catalyst for nurturing compassionate, wise, and globally conscious individuals who will shape a brighter and more harmonious tomorrow for all.

Chapter 8: A Holistic Approach to Health

Health is not merely the absence of illness but a state of harmonious balance in body, mind, and spirit. "A Holistic Approach to Health" invites us to embrace a comprehensive understanding of well-being, integrating physical, mental, and emotional aspects of ourselves. By nurturing our bodies with nourishing food, movement, and rest, we lay the foundation for vitality and vitality.

A holistic approach to health goes beyond focusing solely on physical well-being. It recognizes that our mental and emotional states are equally vital components of our overall health. Inner peace and emotional intelligence are integral to achieving a state of holistic well-being.

In this chapter, we delve into the importance of mental and emotional well-being. We explore practices that promote mindfulness and stress reduction, cultivating a sense of inner tranquility amidst life's challenges. By nurturing emotional intelligence, we learn to understand and regulate our emotions, leading to more balanced and fulfilling lives.

Adopting a holistic approach to health involves self-care practices that sustain us through life's ups and downs. We explore various modalities of self-care, including meditation, yoga, creative expression, and spending time in nature. These practices help us recharge, find balance, and connect with our inner selves.

Furthermore, a holistic approach to health fosters a deep sense of interconnectedness. As we care for ourselves, we recognize that our well-being is intertwined with the well-being of others and the environment. This interconnectedness fuels our motivation to create a healthier world for all beings.

In embracing this comprehensive

understanding of health, we become advocates for a society that prioritizes well-being. A health-focused society is one that values preventative care, mental health support, and holistic healing practices. It is a society where individuals are empowered to take charge of their health, making informed choices that contribute to their overall well-being.

By adopting a holistic approach to health, we sow the seeds for a world where all beings thrive in harmony and balance. This chapter encourages readers to embrace a lifestyle that nourishes their body, mind, and spirit, cultivating a profound sense of well-being that radiates outward, touching the lives of others and the planet we call home.

Chapter 9: Global Collaboration for Positive Change

In a world interconnected by technology and facing numerous global challenges, the need for collaboration has never been more critical. Chapter 9 delves into the concept of uniting as a global community to address pressing issues, share knowledge, and work together toward a more equitable world.

The chapter emphasizes the power of international cooperation, transcending borders and cultural barriers to find solutions for shared problems. It recognizes that no single nation or entity can solve global challenges in isolation. Only through collective efforts can we create a world that ensures a brighter future for all.

At the heart of global collaboration is open communication, empathy, and understanding among nations and cultures. By engaging in dialogue and actively listening to one another, we lay the groundwork for building bridges of cooperation and trust. This understanding fosters unity and paves the way for impactful and sustainable change.

The chapter highlights successful examples of international collaborations that have made a significant impact. Efforts to combat climate change, address poverty and hunger, and promote education and healthcare worldwide showcase the power of collective action in creating positive change.

As technology continues to advance, it plays a crucial role in facilitating global collaboration. The advent of social media, online platforms, and virtual meetings has brought people from different corners of the world closer than ever before. Leveraging these tools becomes vital in promoting positive change and advancing global goals.

While global collaboration offers immense potential for positive change, it is not without its challenges. Cultural differences, conflicting interests, and historical tensions between nations can present obstacles to cooperation. This chapter addresses these challenges head-on, offering insights into fostering stronger and more resilient partnerships.

In conclusion, Chapter 9 emphasizes the urgency and significance of global collaboration in addressing today's most pressing issues. By uniting as a global community, we can harness the power of diversity and cooperation to tackle challenges that transcend borders. Through open communication, empathy, and a shared commitment to positive change, we can build a world that values collaboration and collective progress. By working together, we can create a more equitable, sustainable, and compassionate world for present and future generations.

Chapter 10: Spirituality and Inner Fulfillment

Amidst the pursuit of external achievements and material success, the concept of inner fulfillment and spirituality has been somewhat overlooked. Chapter 10, "Spirituality and Inner Fulfillment," invites us to explore the essence of spirituality and its profound role in finding inner peace and purpose. It delves into various spiritual practices, beliefs, and philosophies from different cultures, showcasing their common threads and how they can lead to a more meaningful life.

At the core of this chapter lies the importance of self-reflection, mindfulness, and understanding one's values and beliefs. By embarking on a journey within, we seek balance and harmony between the physical, mental, and spiritual aspects of our lives. This inward exploration is not confined to any specific religion or creed but rather acknowledges the universal human longing for meaning and connection.

Throughout this chapter, readers will find insights into the potential benefits of incorporating spiritual practices into their daily routines. Whether it's meditation, yoga, prayer, or simply connecting with nature, these practices can help reduce stress, increase resilience, and cultivate a profound sense of gratitude and compassion.

Spirituality also plays a significant role in mental health and well-being. Studies have shown that individuals with a strong spiritual foundation tend to experience better coping mechanisms, lower levels of anxiety and depression, and an increased sense of purpose in life.

Embracing spirituality is not about abandoning the material world, but rather about finding a deeper connection to it. By nurturing our spiritual selves, we become more present, compassionate, and aligned with our true purpose. This sense of inner fulfillment radiates outward, enriching our relationships, communities, and the world.

This chapter also celebrates the diversity

of spiritual beliefs and practices, recognizing that the paths to inner fulfillment are as varied as the human experience itself. By acknowledging the common threads that unite us, we find a shared sense of humanity and interconnectedness.

In conclusion, "Spirituality and Inner Fulfillment" offers a transformative invitation to explore the depths of our inner selves, seeking harmony and purpose. Through spiritual practices and self-reflection, we discover a profound sense of peace and interconnectedness with all living beings. By embracing spirituality as an integral part of our lives, we unlock the potential for inner growth and a deeper connection to the world around us. As we cultivate our spiritual selves, we find the wellspring of inner fulfillment, and from this place of abundance, we can radiate compassion, joy, and love, transforming ourselves and the world for the better.

Chapter 11: Ethical Leadership and Governance

Traditional notions of leadership have

often focused on power, authority, and profit, but Chapter 11, "Ethical Leadership and Governance," challenges this paradigm. The chapter delves into the concept of ethical leadership and explores the qualities and characteristics that define ethical leaders. It emphasizes the importance of empathy, integrity, and accountability in leadership roles.

At the heart of this chapter lies the belief that true

leaders prioritize the collective good over personal gain. Ethical leaders make decisions that consider the well-being of their communities, nations, and the planet as a whole. They cultivate a deep sense of responsibility toward those they lead and seek to inspire positive change for the betterment of all.

Throughout this chapter, readers will find examples of ethical leadership from various fields, such as business, politics, and social activism. These stories showcase how ethical leaders have managed to create positive change and inspire others to follow in their footsteps.

The chapter also explores the impact of ethical governance on institutions and society. Transparency, inclusivity, and fairness become the pillars of ethical governance, creating a just and thriving community. By embracing these principles, organizations and governments can build trust with their constituents and foster a sense of unity and purpose.

Ethical leadership extends beyond individual actions; it lays the groundwork for a culture of integrity and accountability within institutions and societies.

Leaders who uphold ethical standards set a powerful example for those they lead, inspiring a ripple effect of positive change that reaches far beyond their immediate sphere of influence.

Furthermore, the chapter acknowledges the challenges of ethical leadership in a world where conflicting interests and power dynamics often come into play. By addressing these challenges head-on, readers gain insights into building stronger, more resilient ethical leadership practices.

In conclusion, Chapter 11 presents a vision of leadership that goes beyond the pursuit of personal ambition and power. Ethical leaders prioritize collaboration, compassion, and accountability, fostering a world where leadership serves the greater good. By nurturing a new generation of leaders who embrace ethical decision-making and service to the collective, we can create a more harmonious and prosperous world for all. Ethical leadership becomes the catalyst for positive change, uniting diverse voices and visions in pursuit of a shared vision for a brighter future.

Chapter 12: Cosmic Connection

In the vast expanse of Chapter 12, "Cosmic Connection," we embark on a journey beyond the boundaries of our world to explore the wonders of the cosmos and our place within it. Through the lens of science and the marvels of the universe, we come to realize the profound interconnectedness that exists between every particle, planet, and star.

At the heart of this chapter lies the awe-inspiring revelations that come from understanding the grand scale of the universe. We contemplate the billions of galaxies, each containing billions of stars, and the seemingly infinite expanse of space and time. In the face of such vastness, we recognize the humbling truth of our smallness as individuals, yet our integral role in the fabric of the cosmos.

As we gaze up at the stars and contemplate the mysteries of the universe, a profound sense of wonder and humility emerges within us. The cosmic connection we feel stirs a yearning to explore and understand the deepest mysteries of existence. It opens our hearts and minds to the beauty and complexity of life in all its forms.

Moreover, this cosmic perspective leads us to a deeper appreciation for life on our planet. We recognize the delicate balance that sustains life on Earth, and the significance of caring for our home in the vastness of space. The realization that our actions reverberate throughout the cosmos imparts a profound responsibility to protect and preserve the precious ecosystems that nurture life.

As we embrace our cosmic connection, we gain a renewed sense of purpose and interconnectedness with all living beings. This understanding fosters empathy and compassion for others, transcending boundaries of nationality, race, and religion. We realize that, like the stars in the night sky, we are all interconnected and share the same origins.

This cosmic awareness leads us to view our fellow human beings not as strangers but as members of the same cosmic family. It inspires us to build bridges of understanding and cooperation, celebrating the diversity that enriches our collective experience.

In conclusion, "Cosmic Connection" beckons us to explore the wonders of the universe and recognize our place within it. Through this cosmic perspective, we find humility and wonder, realizing the significance of our actions in the grand tapestry of space and time. By embracing our cosmic connection, we nurture a deeper appreciation for life on Earth and foster a sense of interconnectedness with all living beings. This understanding becomes a catalyst for caring for our planet and uniting as a global community in pursuit of a brighter and harmonious future for all.

Chapter 13: Transcending Boundaries

In the vast landscape of Chapter 13, "Transcending Boundaries," we embark on a transformative journey to explore the concept of expanding our perspective and breaking down barriers of fear, prejudice, and separation. This chapter delves into the human tendency to create divisions among ourselves based on race, nationality, religion, and other factors, and how these divisions can lead to conflict and misunderstanding.

At the heart of this chapter lies the profound call to transcend these boundaries and embrace the shared humanity that unites us all. As we shift our focus from the differences that divide us to the common threads that connect us, we cultivate empathy, compassion, and understanding.

The journey of transcending boundaries begins with self-awareness and introspection. We recognize the biases and prejudices within ourselves and actively work to overcome them. By acknowledging our own limitations, we open our hearts to the experiences and perspectives of others.

Through this transformative process, we realize that our shared humanity far outweighs the differences that divide us. We come to understand that every individual, regardless of nationality, race, or belief, seeks happiness, love, and fulfillment in life. This realization sparks a deep sense of interconnectedness with all beings.

Embracing diversity becomes not just a notion but a way of life. We celebrate the richness of cultures, traditions, and beliefs that weave the vibrant tapestry of humanity. In doing so, we foster a sense of unity and cooperation that transcends borders and ideologies.

This unity becomes a powerful force in addressing global

challenges collectively. By working together, we can find innovative solutions to the complex issues that affect us all, from climate change to poverty and beyond. The barriers that once divided us begin to crumble, making way for collaboration and collective progress.

Transcending boundaries also extends beyond human connections. It includes embracing the interconnectedness of all life on Earth. We recognize that our well-being is intrinsically linked to the health of our planet and all its inhabitants. As custodians of the Earth, we hold a shared responsibility to protect and preserve its precious ecosystems.

In conclusion, "Transcending Boundaries" calls us to embark on a transformative journey of breaking down the walls that separate us. By embracing our shared humanity, we nurture empathy, compassion, and understanding. This unity becomes a powerful force for positive change, fostering collaboration and collective progress in addressing global challenges. As we celebrate diversity and cherish our interconnectedness with all living beings, we sow the seeds for a world where unity and harmony prevail, transcending boundaries and transforming humanity for the better.

Chapter 14: Wisdom from Ancient

Traditions

In the timeless realm of Chapter 14, "Wisdom from Ancient Traditions," we embark on a journey to explore the profound insights and teachings passed down through generations from ancient cultures. This chapter delves into the treasure trove of wisdom that offers valuable perspectives on life, spirituality, and the human condition.

At its heart, this chapter emphasizes the significance of learning from the past and drawing from the accumulated wisdom of various cultures. By delving into ancient traditions, readers gain a deeper understanding of human values, ethics, and ways of living that have withstood the test of time. These timeless teachings provide invaluable guidance for navigating the complexities of modern life.

As we immerse ourselves in the wisdom of ancient

cultures, we discover the common threads that unite humanity across time and space. The universal truths and principles found in these traditions transcend cultural boundaries, offering insights into our shared human experience.

This exploration of ancient wisdom invites us to reflect on our own lives and consider how these teachings can be applied to our present circumstances. We find solace in the timeless guidance that can aid us in facing contemporary challenges with grace and resilience.

Moreover, as we embrace the wisdom from ancient traditions, we honor the cultures that have preserved and passed down these profound insights over centuries. It becomes an act of reverence for the wisdom keepers who have safeguarded these teachings and an invitation to continue this legacy for future generations.

In conclusion, "Wisdom from Ancient Traditions" offers a timeless reservoir of insight and guidance for modern times. By delving into the wisdom of our ancestors, we enrich our understanding of life's fundamental truths and embrace the interconnectedness that binds humanity across ages and cultures. This chapter becomes a testament to the enduring value of ancient wisdom, guiding us on a path of wisdom, compassion, and growth as we navigate the ever-changing landscape of existence.

Chapter 15: The Everlasting Journey

In the vast expanse of Chapter 15, "The Everlasting Journey," we embrace the profound notion that life is a continuous journey of growth, evolution, and interconnectedness. This chapter delves into the idea that our existence is an eternal process of learning, discovery, and transformation—a perpetual evolution that connects all beings in the grand tapestry of existence.

At its core, this chapter encourages readers to embrace change, personal growth, and the cyclical nature of life. We recognize that each experience, whether joyous or challenging, contributes to our evolution as individuals and as a collective. The ebb and flow of life's experiences become the rhythm of our journey, shaping us into the individuals we are meant to become.

As we journey through life, we find that

growth is not linear but a continuous spiral of self-discovery and expansion. We celebrate the beauty of embracing impermanence, knowing that change is a constant and that each moment carries the potential for new beginnings.

This everlasting journey also fosters a sense of interconnectedness with all living beings. We recognize that we are not isolated entities but intricately connected threads in the cosmic fabric of existence. By understanding our interconnectedness, we find compassion and empathy for others, realizing that their journeys, too, are intertwined with our own.

In embracing the everlasting journey, we find purpose and meaning in the continuous flow of life. We release the burden of striving for a static destination and find joy in the journey itself. Each step becomes a moment of presence and gratitude as we navigate the uncharted waters of existence.

Moreover, this journey of eternal growth extends beyond our individual lives. It encompasses the collective evolution of humanity, as we navigate challenges and celebrate triumphs as a global community. We recognize that our collective journey is an opportunity for shared growth and co-creation.

In conclusion, "The Everlasting Journey" invites us to embrace the dynamic nature of life, recognizing it as an eternal process of growth and interconnectedness. By embracing change, personal growth, and the cyclical nature of existence, we find purpose and meaning in the journey itself. As we honor the continuity of life's evolution, we cultivate compassion, unity, and resilience. The everlasting journey becomes a profound celebration of life, connection, and the infinite possibilities that unfold as we traverse the vastness of existence.

Conclusion: Illuminating the Path Ahead - Reflecting on the transformative power of unity and interconnectedness, and how we can shape a harmonious future.

As the final thread is woven into the fabric of "Evolving Unity," we stand in awe of the cosmic symphony that connects us all. From the vastness of space to the depths of our hearts, we are united by the common thread of existence. In unity, we find strength, compassion, and the courage to face the challenges that lie ahead.

Throughout this journey, we have encountered the transformative power of recognizing our cosmic connection, breaking down barriers, learning from ancient wisdom, and embracing the everlasting journey. The lessons of unity and interconnectedness resonate deeply within us, inspiring a renewed sense of purpose and hope.

In this concluding chapter, we envision a future where humanity, like the stars in the night sky, shines brightly in harmony. Together, we are a force of positive change, capable of healing our planet and building bridges of understanding across borders and divides. Let this book serve as a guiding light, illuminating the path ahead as we navigate the ever-evolving tapestry of life.

Acknowledgments: Gratitude for the Collective Effort - Recognizing the contributions of all those who have played a part in bringing "Evolving Unity" to life.

In this symphony of unity, we extend our deepest gratitude to all those who have contributed to the realization of "Evolving Unity." To our dedicated team of researchers, editors, and supporters, thank you for lending your brilliance and passion to this endeavor. To the countless individuals whose stories and experiences have enriched our narrative, we express our heartfelt appreciation.

To the readers who embark on this transformative journey with us, your open minds and open hearts fuel the optimism and confidence in the scriptures we present. It is through the collective effort and collaboration of each soul that this book has come to light, illuminating the path towards a more harmonious world.

Appendix: Tools for Unity and Action - Practical

resources and tools to inspire readers to take meaningful steps towards unity and positive change.

As we near the conclusion of this cosmic voyage, we offer you a guidebook, an Appendix filled with practical tools for unity and action. Here, you will find tangible steps and resources to cultivate empathy, break down barriers, and foster a spirit of togetherness. We encourage you to explore these tools with an open heart and implement them in your lives and communities.

May this appendix empower you to become catalysts for positive transformation, igniting the flame of unity within your circles and beyond.

Remember, your actions ripple through the cosmos, and by embracing unity, you become part of a profound movement to create a brighter, harmonious future for all.

About the Author: A Catalyst for Unity

Meet the author of "Evolving Unity," a passionate soul on a mission to foster unity and interconnectedness in the world. Through personal experiences and profound insights, the author has woven a tapestry of wisdom that resonates with the hearts of readers.

Driven by an unwavering belief in the transformative power of unity, the author has dedicated their life to inspiring others to embrace the cosmic connection that unites us all. With deep humility and boundless optimism, the author invites you to join them on this eternal journey towards unity and understanding.

Glossary: Key Concepts and Terms

1. Cosmic Connection: The recognition and understanding of our interconnectedness with the vast cosmos,

acknowledging that we are an integral part of the universe and its cosmic dance.

2. Unity: The state of being united, interconnected, and in harmony with oneself, others, and the world around us. It involves recognizing our shared humanity and working towards common goals.

3. Interconnectedness: The understanding that everything in the universe is interconnected and that actions and events in one

part of the system can have consequences for other parts. It highlights the idea that we are all connected on a fundamental level.

4. Empathy: The ability to understand and

share the feelings and experiences of others. It involves putting ourselves in someone else's shoes and cultivating compassion and understanding.

5. Compassion: Deep empathy and care for the well-being of others. It involves a willingness to alleviate suffering and promote kindness and understanding in the world.

6. Diversity: The range of different individuals, ideas, cultures, and perspectives

that exist in the world. Embracing diversity involves recognizing the value and richness that comes from differences and fostering inclusivity.

7. Transcendence: The act of rising above limitations or boundaries, whether physical, emotional, or spiritual. It involves going beyond preconceived notions and expanding our understanding to reach a higher level of consciousness.

8. Wisdom: A deep understanding and insight into fundamental truths about life, the universe, and human existence. Wisdom is often gained through experience, reflection, and the pursuit of

knowledge.

9. Interfaith Dialogue: The respectful and open exchange of ideas, beliefs, and practices among individuals from different religious traditions. It seeks to promote understanding, cooperation, and harmony among diverse religious communities.

10. Sustainability: The practice of living in a way that meets the needs of the present generation without compromising the ability of

future generations to meet their own needs. It involves balancing environmental, social, and economic considerations for long-term well-being.

11. Mindfulness: The practice of being fully present and aware in the current moment, without judgment. It involves cultivating a deep sense of attention and focus to enhance self-awareness and connection with the world.

12. Harmony: The state of peaceful coexistence, balance, and integration. It involves finding a synergistic relationship between different elements, whether in nature, society, or within oneself.

13. Transformation: The process of profound and lasting change, often resulting in personal growth, enlightenment, or a shift in consciousness. It involves letting go of old patterns and embracing new possibilities.

14. Global Citizenship: The recognition that we are all members of a global community, with responsibilities and rights that extend beyond national borders. It involves actively engaging in creating a more

just, peaceful, and
sustainable world.

15. Intergenerational
Wisdom: The knowledge,
experiences, and insights
passed down from one
generation to the next. It
emphasizes the importance
of learning from the past
and honoring the wisdom of
previous generations.

16. Interconnected Web of
Life: The recognition that all
living beings, ecosystems,
and natural processes are
interconnected and
interdependent. It highlights

the delicate balance and harmony that sustains life on Earth.

17. Positive Change: The intentional and proactive efforts to create beneficial and

transformative outcomes in individuals, communities, and the world. It involves taking action towards a more inclusive, just, and sustainable future.

18. Resilience: The capacity to adapt, recover, and bounce back from challenges, setbacks, or adversity. It involves cultivating inner strength and resourcefulness to navigate and thrive in the face of change.

19. Empowerment: The process of enabling individuals or communities to gain control over their lives, make choices, and take actions that lead to personal and collective growth. It involves fostering autonomy, confidence, and agency.

20. Interdependent Coexistence: The recognition that all beings, systems, and elements of existence rely on one another for mutual support and survival. It emphasizes the understanding that our

well-being is interconnected with the well-being of others and the planet.

As you delve deeper into the concepts explored in "Evolving Unity," may this glossary serve as a guiding companion, illuminating the path and fostering a shared understanding as we journey towards unity and interconnectedness.

www.ingramcontent.com/pod-product-compliance
Lightning Source LLC
Chambersburg PA
CBHW072158290526
45794CB00004B/1565